by Jessica Strand

photographs by Laurie Frankel

holiday cocktails

CHRONICLE BOOKS

SAN FRANCISCO

For Stephen, who not only guides me through life, but also shakes the meanest cocktail around.

acknowledgments Most of all I'd like to thank my husband, Stephen Tseckares, who took on this project with me, shaking, stirring, and blending all through the holiday season. He is the best mixologist I know. A giant thanks to all those amazing folks at Chronicle Books who helped move this project along so speedily. Thank you Lisa Campbell, Ben Shaykin, Pamela Geismar, Doug Ogan, Beth Steiner, and Jan Hughes. And in particular my editor, the talented, generous Leslie Jonath, whose encouragement and enthusiasm not only is infectious but also makes her writers want to work their hardest. A big thanks to Laurie Frankel, whose glamorous photographs and design make this book a visual celebration, and to Sharilyn Hovind, who carefully edited my prose. Many thanks to all those wonderful friends who helped test various libations. And a special thank you to my sweet, patient son, who never complains when Mommy's got to work—thank you, little bean.

the photographer gratefully acknowledges: Calvin Klein Home (877)256.7373, Egg (415)564.2248, Gumps (800)766.7628, Hammonds Candies (303)333.5588, J. Goldsmith Antiques (415)567.2440, Recchiuti Confections (415)826.2868, Pomp Home (415)864.1830, Pottery Barn, Propeller (415)701.7767, Sur La Table (510)849.2252, Sue Fisher King (415)922.7276, The Gardner (510)548.4545, and Laura Fergason, for their lovely props. To Robyn Valarik, Alessandra Mortola, Toby Hanson, Leslie Jonath, Lisa Campbell, Ben Shaykin, Pamela Geismar, Tera Killip, Tracy Astle, and Kristie Oaks for all their time and talents.

Text copyright © 2003 by Jessica Strand.
Photographs copyright © 2003 by Laurie Frankel.

Library of Congress Cataloging-in-Publication Data:
Strand, Jessica.
Holiday cocktails / by Jessica Strand; photographs by Laurie Frankel p. cm.
ISBN 0-8118-4157-X (Hardcover)
1. Cocktails. 2. Holiday cookery. I. Title.
TX951.S89 2003   641.8'74–dc21

Manufactured in Canada

www.chroniclebooks.com

Prop styling by Alessandra Mortola, Robyn Valarik, and Toby Hanson
Food styling by Robyn Valarik
Designed by Laurie Frankel

Distributed in Canada by Raincoast Books
9050 Shaughnessy Street
Vancouver, British Columbia V6P 6E5

10 9 8 7 6 5 4 3 2

Chronicle Books LLC
85 Second Street
San Francisco, California 94105

Angostura bitters is a registered trademark of Angostura International. Baileys Irish Cream is a registered trademark of R&A Bailey & Com., Limited. Bombay Sapphire is a registered trademark of Bacardi and Company Ltd. Chambord is a registered trademark of Chatam International Inc. Clamato is a registered trademark of CBI Holdings Inc. Kahlúa is a registered trademark of The Kahlúa Company. Tabasco Sauce is a registered trademark of McIlhenny Company.

contents

recipes

indexes

introduction

I love when the weather turns from cool to chilly, the days grow shorter, and our family gears up for the holiday season. We hang a wreath on the door, trim a tree with yards of flickering lights, and tack mistletoe to the most traveled doorway in our home. With this winter decorating comes the fun of planning holiday parties: My husband pulls out his favorite seasonal tunes, I turn up the heat, he stokes the fire, and we open our doors to friends and family for heartwarming food and festive drinks.

That's where this book comes in. Here, you'll find more than fifty recipes for classic holiday drinks, as well as clever new concoctions that may quickly become favorites. I hope that among them, you'll find holiday cheer and perhaps even inspiration for a party theme. You can let your libations set the tone at a sophisticated martini party, homey post-shopping get-together, or romantic tête-à-tête on a snowy night.

All of the recipes in this book emphasize the celebratory nature of the holiday season with strong flavors and striking colors. Very Merry Cocktails are fun, festive drinks, made to order. Perhaps you'd like an Evergreen (page 21), a rich, minty tequila concoction dusted with freshly ground cocoa, or maybe an Apple Snowflake Martini (page 22), a fruity, slightly tart, green-colored cocktail topped with a crisp apple slice.

Champagne Sippers suit the most glamorous occasions; consider a ruby-toned Kir Royale (page 44) for a romantic aperitif on Christmas Eve, or a tray of Holiday Bellinis (page 38) to ring in the new year. Hot toddies, on the other hand, lend a comforting, homespun touch. Hot Mint Chocolate (page 50), made with peppermint schnapps, is welcomed après-ski or caroling on a cold winter's night.

Perfect for a crowd, Holiday Punches are simple to make and encourage mingling around the punch bowl. This section offers a range of choices, from Classic Eggnog (page 67), to spicy Wassail (page 62).

For nondrinkers and kids, Lively (Nonalcoholic) Libations will make sure they don't feel left out of the party. Offer them a quenching Gingersnap Punch (page 73), made with ginger ale, raspberry syrup, and lime juice, or a rich Foamy Mexican Hot Chocolate (page 70) with a dollop of fresh whipped cream.

Enjoy the holidays, sit back and relax. Mix a cocktail for yourself and a friend and toast to the season and all the joy it brings. Cheers! Happy holidays to one and all!

bar equipment

Here's a simple list of bar tools that are particularly useful for making these holiday cocktails and other drinks.

Bar Spoon: This long-handled spoon is ideal for stirring drinks in a mixing glass, serving glass, or pitcher.

Bar Strainer: This coil-rimmed strainer is necessary for straining ice out of a mixing glass or shaker.

Bar Towel: Not only a practical accessory for wiping up spills, decorative bar towels can help you bring the holiday theme into any party.

Citrus Reamer/Squeezer: When you're entertaining, you don't want friends to line up for a drink while you struggle to get the last bits of juice out of your citrus. These tools speed up the job.

Cocktail Shaker/Mixing Glass: This is an essential two-part item for shaking cocktails. The mixing glass serves as your container for stirred, not shaken cocktails.

Corkscrew: A basic item for any bar. Though it's typically not needed for mixing cocktails, be sure to have one on hand for recipes that require wine, like Glögg (page 66).

Ice Bucket and Tongs: A bucket can be both a decorative and useful item to store your ice during a party so it won't melt. It can be nice to have an extra pair of tongs set out so two guests can fill their glasses at the same time.

Ice Pick/Mallet: It's nice to have to have something on hand to break up the ice, but, it's certainly not essential if you are using ice cubes.

Jigger Measure/Shot Glass: This is an extremely handy item to have around, particularly for less experienced mixologists. Look for one that has half-ounce gradations to help you measure accurately.

Picks: Wooden, plastic, metal, or bamboo skewers can add a delightful touch to all kinds of garnishes. Have a variety on hand to complement the different styles of glassware in your collection.

Vegetable Peeler: Use this indispensable tool to create a twist of lemon, lime, or any other fruit with a hard skin.

Zester/Stripper: This is a very helpful tool that strips the rind from fruits for garnishes.

stocking the holiday bar

Because you'll be entertaining more, you'll want to stock up your bar for the holidays. The following lists include items you'll need for mixing drinks at this festive time of year. Personalize your bar by noting the kinds of drinks you and your guests prefer and choosing some fun seasonal garnishes—browse through the recipes in this book for ideas! Buy enough supplies so that you'll be prepared for drop-in visitors and last minute get-togethers.

Holiday Mixers and Ingredients

Below you'll find two lists—Essentials and Extras—to help you prepare for the holiday rush. The Essentials give you the basics you need to make a wide variety of cocktails, while the Extras prepare you to whip up any of the recipes in this book.

Essentials

Angostura bitters
Clamato
Club soda or seltzer
Cocoa
Coffee
Crème de cassis
Fruit juices such as apple cider,
    apricot nectar, cranberry, lemonade,
    mango, orange
Ginger ale
Grenadine
Heavy whipping cream, half-and-half,
    and whole milk
Ice
Lemons, limes, and oranges,
    for juicing

Sugar: brown, dark brown,
    confectioners, and superfine
Vanilla extract
Water

Extras

Black pepper, freshly ground
Blanched whole almonds
Butter
Cardamom pods
Creamed horseradish
Eggs
Malted milk powder
Maple syrup
Mexican hot chocolate
Salt
Sugar cubes
Tabasco
Worcestershire sauce

Holiday Liquors

There are many brands of liquor, and you will typically find the more you spend, the smoother and better the taste. That's not to say that a less expensive alcohol will ruin a drink—do your own taste tests to decide for yourself. Consider purchasing larger bottles to get a better deal on a tastier brand. And don't worry about the spoilage, since bottled spirits have an infinite shelf life.

Essentials

Brandy

Champagne

Cream liqueurs: Irish cream, such as
Bailey's; coffee liqueur, such as
Kahlúa

Gin

Light and dark rum

Orange liqueur such as Cointreau or
Triple Sec

Red wine

Schnapps: butterscotch, peppermint,
sour apple

Sweet and dry vermouth

Tequila

Vodka

Extras

Aquavit

Blue curaçao

Bombay Sapphire gin

Calvados

Campari

Cordials: crème de cacao, amaretto,
crème de menthe, Chambord, ouzo

Currant vodka

Irish whiskey

Lillet

Midori

Muscat dessert wine

Peach liquor

Pear eau de vie

Holiday Garnishes

From lemon twists to mini candy canes and cinnamon sticks, garnishes create the mood of a drink. Most of these just take seconds to prepare, while others are more elaborate. They all add holiday flavor and festivity. Here is a list to get you thinking, and remember that some garnishes can alter the flavor of the drink, so be sure to test your own creations before serving them to a crowd.

Flavored Rims

Candied Citrus Slices (page 8)

Chocolate Rim (page 8)

Cinnamon Rim (page 9)

Cocoa Rim (page 9)

Sugar Rim (page 9)

Sugared Apple Slices (page 9)

Sweet and Savory Additions

Almond shavings

Cinnamon sticks

Citrus wedges: lemon, lime, orange

Cocoa

Cucumbers

Edible herbs and flowers, such as
lemon balm, rose petals, rosemary,
tarragon, basil, lavender, marigolds,
nasturtiums, begonias, violets

Frozen blueberries

Frozen melon balls

Gold leaf

Grapes

Mangos

Maraschino cherries

Mini candy canes

Mint sprig

Nutmeg

Olives

Pearl onions

Pears

Pomegranate seeds

Tiny silver and gold candy balls

garnish recipes

Candied Citrus Slices/Citrus Syrup

This recipe provides two ingredients at once. While you're candying your citrus fruit, you'll also be making a delightful citrus syrup. Feel free to candy any type of citrus fruit including tangerines, lemons, limes, grapefruit, oranges, or kumquats.

1 cup sugar	2 lemons, 2 limes, 1 orange, or 1
½ cup water	grapefruit, cut into ⅛-inch
	slices or rounds

Combine sugar and water in a saucepan and bring to a boil. Cut the citrus you are using into ⅛-inch slices, and add to pan. Let the boiling syrup reduce for 5 minutes or until it begins to thicken, turning citrus occasionally. Pull citrus slices out and place on a piece of wax paper to cool. Cool citrus syrup on the stove. Store covered in the refrigerator when cool. Citrus slices will last for 2 to 3 days in the refrigerator. The citrus syrup will keep almost indefinitely.

Chocolate Rim

6 oz bittersweet or semi-sweet chocolate, chopped finely or chips	3 tbsp heavy whipping cream
	1 tbsp butter

In a double boiler, melt the chocolate over just-simmering water, stirring until smooth. (Make sure the top pan sits over, not in, the water.) Add the cream and butter and stir until smooth. Remove top pan and let chocolate sit for 2 to 3 minutes. Quickly dip the rim of a glass in the chocolate, remove, and let excess drip off. Turn over the prepared glass and place immediately in the refrigerator for at least ½ hour. Makes 8 to 10 chocolate rims.

Cranberry Wreath

Wreaths speak of the holiday season. Why not decorate a cocktail with one, too! Here's a recipe for your very own cranberry wreath. Note: This wreath is not edible.

One 5½-inch thin piece, pliable wire	15 to 20 dried cranberries

Cut a piece of thin pliable 5½-inch wire. String cranberries across the piece of wire until it's covered. Bend the wire without joining the ends, making a circular "wreath," and then hook onto the side of a glass.

Sugared Apple Slices

It's important when slicing the apple to make sure it's about a $\frac{1}{16}$ of an inch thick, thin enough to float rather than sink. Feel free to substitute a hard pear, like a Bosc.

1 tart green apple, such as Granny Smith or pippin	Superfine sugar

Quarter and core apple. Cut quarters into very thin slices. Place sugar on a small plate. Coat both sides of apple slice in sugar, shaking gently to remove excess sugar. Use immediately.

Sugar/Cocoa/Cinnamon/Kosher-Salt Rim

Choose your glass. (If you want a frosted glass combined with a decorative rim, chill the glass first in the freezer for about an hour.) On a small plate wider than the edge of the rim of the glass, pour a shallow layer of superfine sugar, cocoa, cinnamon, or kosher salt. Wet the rim of the glass with a slice of orange, lemon, or lime or just with a little water (use a lightly dampened paper towel), then dip the rim evenly in the garnish. Lift and tap lightly to remove excess before turning glass over.

Variation: Use cinnamon flavored sugar or colored sugar.

Sugar Syrup

Once you begin blending your cocktails, you will find sugar syrup to be essential. Granulated sugar doesn't dissolve easily in cold drinks, but sugar syrup is already liquid. It's also a breeze to make. As a rule of thumb, recipe measurements of sugar syrup and granulated sugar are interchangeable.

4 cups sugar	2 cups water

Put the sugar and water in a saucepan and bring to a boil over medium heat, stirring continuously as the sugar dissolves. Turn heat down to medium-low. Dip a brush in hot water and wipe down the sides of the pan where crystals may be clinging. Boil for another 3 minutes, then remove from heat. Let the syrup cool and refrigerate in a covered container. The sugar syrup will last almost indefinitely.

very merry cocktails

Mix, shake, and garnish. Repeat! Here's a collection of celebratory cocktails that will add a special touch to any seasonal gathering. Friends are always intrigued and excited when you offer an unusual drink, and what better time to offer one than during the holidays. Your guests will enjoy these playful libations adorned with fun, festive garnishes—like a Christmas Cosmo with a miniature cranberry wreath (page 18), or a Candy Cane Martini finished with a tiny candy cane (page 28). So grab your cocktail shaker and your favorite glass, and get started.

Chocolate Kiss, page 21

silver bell martini

"Silver bells, silver bells…" This glamorous drink (pictured right) perfectly captures the elegance of that holiday standard.

2 oz dry gin
¼ oz dry vermouth

Pearl onions, 2 or 3,
for garnish
Silver candy balls, for garnish

Pour gin and vermouth over ice in a mixing glass. Stir vigorously until cold, then strain into a chilled martini glass. Place pearl onions on a toothpick and drop into drink, then add a few silver candy balls. MAKES 1 DRINK.

it's a wonderful life

If only George Bailey could have sipped one of these smooth, creamy cocktails. He would have known right away what a wonderful life he had.

3 oz half-and-half
1½ oz Irish cream
liqueur

½ oz crème de menthe
Cinnamon, for garnish

Pour half-and-half, Irish cream liqueur, and crème de menthe over a handful of ice in a cocktail shaker. Shake until cold, then strain into an old-fashioned glass half filled with ice. Dust with cinnamon. MAKES 1 DRINK.

winter sunset

This pale tangerine cocktail will remind you of a pretty winter sunset. You can adjust the relative tartness or sweetness by the amount of lemon syrup and grenadine you use.

1½ oz gin

½ oz dry vermouth

½ oz freshly squeezed lemon juice

1 tsp lemon syrup (page 8), at room temperature, or to taste

½ tsp grenadine, or to taste

Candied lemon slice (page 8), for garnish

Pour gin, vermouth, and lemon juice over a handful of ice in a cocktail shaker. Shake until very cold, then strain into a chilled martini glass. Add lemon syrup and grenadine, then gently stir with a bar spoon. Drop in candied lemon slice; it should sink, creating a yellow line around the glass—the setting sun.

MAKES 1 DRINK.

meyer lemon margarita

This variation on the margarita uses Meyer lemons instead of limes. A Meyer lemon is a large thick-skinned lemon that tastes like a cross between a sweet lemon and an orange. If you can't find them, then substitute ¼ oz freshly squeezed orange juice plus ¾ oz freshly squeezed lemon juice. You'll find this a little more tart than your classic margarita.

Meyer lemon wedge,
    for rim
Kosher salt, for rim
1½ oz tequila

½ oz orange liqueur
1 oz freshly squeezed
    Meyer lemon juice
Lemon round, for garnish

Wet the rim of a martini glass with lemon wedge and dip rim in salt to coat. Tap gently to shake off excess. Pour tequila, orange liqueur, and lemon juice over a handful of ice in a cocktail shaker. Shake until cold, then pour drink into prepared glass. Garnish with a lemon round. MAKES 1 DRINK.

starry night

Here's a smooth, creamy drink that will make you see stars you've never seen before—so watch out!

Cocoa, for rim
2 oz vodka
1 oz coffee liqueur

1 oz Irish cream liqueur
3 coffee beans, for garnish

Wet rim of a martini glass with water or room-temperature coffee, and dip in cocoa to coat. Pour vodka, coffee liqueur, and Irish cream liqueur over a handful of ice in a cocktail shaker. Shake until cold, then strain into prepared glass. Top with coffee beans. MAKES 1 DRINK.

flickering lights

Brandy devotees might recognize the sting in this drink, also known as a "Stinger." Although overlooked in recent years, it is a good drink for the holidays.

1½ oz brandy
½ oz crème de menthe

Piece of goldleaf,
for garnish

Pour brandy and crème de menthe over a handful of ice in a cocktail shaker. Shake until cold, then strain into a martini glass. Garnish with goldleaf. MAKES 1 DRINK.

christmas cosmo

Adorn this playful pink concoction (pictured right) with a tiny cranberry wreath for an extra holiday touch.

1 oz currant vodka

½ oz orange liqueur

1 tsp freshly squeezed
   lime juice

½ oz cranberry juice

Lime wedge, for garnish

Tiny cranberry wreath
   (page 8), for garnish

Pour vodka, orange liqueur, lime juice, and cranberry juice over a handful of ice in a cocktail shaker. Shake until very cold. Strain into a chilled martini glass or other chilled glass. Garnish with lime wedge as desired. MAKES 1 DRINK.

the snowplow

This refreshing winter cocktail is made with aquavit, a clear Scandinavian liquor made from grain or potatoes and flavored with the nutty, anise-tasting caraway seed.

1 oz aquavit

6 oz lemonade

Lemon slice, for garnish

Fill a highball glass with ice. Add aquavit and lemonade, then stir. Set lemon slice on rim. MAKES 1 DRINK.

the evergreen

Cream adds a rich, smooth consistency to this tequila cocktail (pictured left), but beware—it packs a punch.

1 oz tequila

1 oz heavy whipping cream

1 oz crème de cacao

½ oz crème de menthe

Chocolate sprinkles, for garnish

Pour tequila, cream, crème de cacao, and crème de menthe over a handful of ice in a cocktail shaker. Shake until very cold, then strain into a chilled martini glass or other footed glass, rimmed with chocolate sprinkles. MAKES 1 DRINK.

chocolate kiss

Although this is a chocolate martini, it's not overly sweet. Don't leave out the orange—without it, the drink isn't as good.

Orange wedge, for rim

Cocoa, for rim

1½ oz vodka

½ oz crème de cacao

Chocolate candy, for garnish

Wet the rim of a martini glass with orange wedge and dip rim in cocoa to coat. Pour vodka and crème de cacao over a handful of ice in a cocktail shaker. Shake until cold, then strain into a prepared glass. Drop chocolate candy into the bottom of the glass, for garnish, if desired. MAKES 1 DRINK.

apple snowflake martini

Think of the light, crystalline frost that creates beautiful snowflake patterns on the windows in winter. After you've shaken and poured this martini into a glass, you'll notice the tiny residue of ice scattering over the top in the same snowflake pattern.

1 oz vodka

1 oz sour apple schnapps

1 oz apple juice

Sugared apple slice, for garnish

Pour vodka, sour apple schnapps, and apple juice over a handful of ice in a cocktail shaker. Shake until very cold, then strain into a chilled, tall glass. Place apple slice in glass for garnish. You can also serve this in a martini glass and place the apple slice on top. MAKES 1 DRINK.

rudolph's red cocktail

As soon as this bubbly libation (pictured left) touches your lips, you'll know the holidays are here.

Sugar cube	4 oz champagne
Drop of Angostura bitters	Splash of Campari

Place sugar cube in champagne flute or other footed glass. Drop Angostura bitters onto sugar cube. Add champagne and Campari. MAKES 1 DRINK.

the snowball

This is a variation on the classic made with anisette. I've substituted ouzo, which provides the same licorice flavor without quite as much sweetness. Serve it in the roundest glass possible—it is a Snowball after all!

1½ oz gin	1 tbsp half-and-half
½ oz ouzo	

Pour gin, ouzo, and half-and-half over a handful of ice in a cocktail shaker. Shake until very cold, then strain into a chilled, small red wineglass (or any similarly round glass). MAKES 1 DRINK.

white christmas

This creamy drink (pictured right) could pass for melted ice cream if it weren't for the little kick at the end.

1 oz vodka

1 oz amaretto

1 oz heavy whipping cream

Freshly grated nutmeg, for garnish

Pour vodka, amaretto, and cream over a handful of ice in a cocktail shaker. Shake until cold, then strain into a chilled martini glass. Grate a little touch of nutmeg on top. MAKES 1 DRINK.

naughty and nice

Here's my version of the bittersweet Negroni cocktail. Instead of serving it over ice with a dash of club soda, I prefer it shaken and served in a martini glass.

1 oz gin

1 oz Campari

1 oz sweet vermouth

Lemon twist, for garnish

Maraschino cherry, for garnish

Pour gin, Campari, and vermouth over a handful of ice in a cocktail shaker. Shake until very cold, then pour into a chilled martini glass. Twist lemon peel over the glass, then drop in. Add a maraschino cherry. MAKES 1 DRINK.

candy cane martini

Here's a martini (pictured right) that goes down like candy. The mini candy cane adds the perfect holiday touch.

1½ oz vodka	1 oz club soda
1 tsp peppermint schnapps	Mini candy cane, for garnish

Pour vodka, peppermint schnapps, and club soda over a handful of ice in a cocktail shaker. Shake until cold, then pour into a chilled martini glass. Hang mini candy cane over lip of glass. MAKES 1 DRINK.

feliz navidad

This bold blue drink adds a touch of Mexico to any holiday bash. "Feliz Navidad, Feliz Navidad..."

1 oz blue curaçao	4 oz champagne
1 oz tequila	Orange slice, for garnish
1 oz freshly squeezed lime juice	Lemon verbena or lemon balm sprig, for garnish

Pour blue curaçao, tequila, lime juice, and champagne into a red wineglass filled with 4 to 5 ice cubes. Stir with bar spoon, then garnish with orange slice and lemon verbena or lemon balm. MAKES 1 DRINK.

santa's surprise

The chocolate rim on this dessert drink (pictured left) makes for a beautiful presentation and a bit more chocolate flavor in every sip, but isn't necessary to create a delicious drink.

2 oz coffee liqueur	2 oz peppermint schnapps

Chill a glass of your choice and prepare with a chocolate rim (see page 8). Pour coffee liqueur and peppermint schnapps over a handful of ice in a cocktail shaker. Shake until cold, then strain into a prepared glass. MAKES 1 DRINK.

bonne fête fizz

Yes, it's a classic Gin Fizz, that cocktail people have been sipping for generations. It's an effervescent, nose tickling drink that's perfect for the holidays.

1 tbsp confectioners' sugar or sugar syrup (page 9)	Soda water
Juice of ½ lemon	Cucumber, peeled and sliced diagonally, for garnish
2 oz gin	Lemon round, for garnish

In a highball glass filled with ice, add sugar, lemon juice, and gin. Fill remainder of glass with soda water. Stir vigorously. Garnish with cucumber and lemon. MAKES 1 DRINK.

mrs. claus

Santa may be the one circling the globe on a sled, but Mrs. Claus needs to relax, too. Here's the recipe (pictured left) she enjoys with her favorite elf.

3¼ oz gin
¾ oz orange liqueur

1⅛ oz freshly squeezed lemon juice
1 egg white (see Note, page 67)

Pour gin, orange liqueur, lemon juice, and egg white over a handful of ice in a cocktail shaker. Shake until very cold, then strain into martini glass or other chilled glass. MAKES 2 DRINKS.

scroogedriver

Here's a classic that never goes out of fashion. And though Tiny Tim may find it a bit potent, it's divine at brunch or as an evening holiday cocktail.

1½ oz vodka
5 oz freshly squeezed orange juice

Mini Christmas ball on hook, for decoration

Pour vodka and orange juice into a highball filled with ice. Hook mini Christmas ball to outside of glass. MAKES 1 DRINK.

the grinch

This drink gets its name from its bright green color—just like the Grinch himself. Its subtle melon flavor makes it a wonderful aperitif or a nice light drink to sip by the fire.

½ oz freshly squeezed
   lemon juice

1 tsp sugar syrup (page 8)

2 oz Midori

Frozen melon ball, or
   maraschino cherry, for
   garnish

Pour lemon juice, sugar syrup, and Midori over a handful of ice in a cocktail shaker. Shake until cold, then strain into a chilled martini glass. Garnish with a frozen melon ball or maraschino cherry. MAKES 1 DRINK.

champagne sippers

Whether you serve it at a Christmas Day brunch or on New Year's Eve, there's no other beverage that marks a celebration like champagne. Ah, those lovely light bubbles dancing on your tongue! Not only is uncorking an event, but the sparkling effervescence of the drink makes it a true party-pleaser.

Pear Champagne Cocktail, page 40

santa baby

Ring in the New Year with this delightful crimson cocktail (pictured right). Every time you take a sip, pomegranate seeds will rise and fall, dancing in the champagne bubbles.

½ oz Chambord
5 oz champagne

5 to 6 pomegranate seeds

Pour Chambord into a champagne flute or other tall glass, then add champagne. Finish by dropping the seeds into the cocktail. MAKES 1 DRINK.

holiday bellini

Here's a winter version of the famous classic that originated at Harry's Bar in Venice. Instead of fresh white peaches, this recipe uses apricot nectar.

1 oz apricot nectar, chilled
4 oz chilled champagne

Cranberry wreath
(page 8), for garnish

Pour apricot nectar into a champagne flute. Fill to the top with champagne and stir. Hook cranberry wreath to outside of glass. MAKES 1 DRINK.

pear champagne cocktail

This fresh, wintry cocktail works only if both the pear liqueur and champagne are well chilled. If you like, rim the glass with citrus juice and dip in sugar.

1 oz pear eau de vie	Frozen pear wedge,
4 to 5 oz champagne	for garnish, or strip of pear

Pour pear eau de vie into a champagne flute. Fill the rest of the glass with champagne. Garnish with a frozen pear wedge. MAKES 1 DRINK.

a peachy present

An ultrafeminine cocktail to pour your beloved (or have your beloved pour you) on New Year's Eve. The bow says it all. Cheers!

Peach-colored silk ribbon,	5 oz champagne
for decoration	Mint sprig, for garnish
½ oz peach liqueur	

Tie ribbon around the bowl of a red wineglass. Make a tight knot, then tie a medium-size bow. Cut the ends of the ribbon. Pour peach liqueur into glass, then add champagne. Stir gently. Garnish with mint sprig. MAKES 1 DRINK.

french kiss

This cocktail uses Lillet, a French aperitif made from herbs, wine, and brandy. Its distinctive flavor adds sophistication to this delicate cocktail. It is the perfect romantic drink with which to toast the new year.

1 oz Lillet
4 oz champagne

Orange twist, for garnish

Pour Lillet into a champagne flute. Add champagne and stir. Twist orange peel over drink and drop in. MAKES 1 DRINK.

the elf

Part of the beauty of this cocktail is its lime-green color, and the sugared rim resembles snow crystals, giving it an even more seasonal look. The delicate melon flavor goes perfectly with prosciutto.

Lime wedge, for rim
3 tsp superfine sugar,
    for rim

½ oz Midori
5 oz champagne

Wet the rim of a champagne flute with lime wedge and dip rim in sugar to coat. Pour Midori into glass, then add champagne. Stir. MAKES 1 DRINK.

christmas morning mango mimosa

Here's a spin on an orange mimosa. This light, tropical variation is also excellent with brunch, as well as being a lovely aperitif.

Cubed mango (4 to 5 small cubes)	1 oz mango juice
	4 oz champagne

Place cubed mango in a champagne flute. Pour mango juice and champagne over a handful of ice in a cocktail shaker. Shake until cold, then strain into flute. MAKES 1 DRINK.

Variation: Create mimosas for a crowd by multiplying the recipe by the number of guests and straining the mango juice and champagne mixture into a pitcher.

kir royale

This lovely aperitif gets its pale cranberry hue from
crème de cassis, a black currant–flavored liqueur first
produced by the French in Burgundy. Choose a champagne with a taste you enjoy. The crème de cassis will
impart a delicate berry essence to your cocktail. You
can add a little lime juice to temper the sweetness,
if you like.

½ oz crème de cassis

½ tsp freshly squeezed
   lime juice (optional)

Sugar rim (page 9),
   for garnish

5 oz champagne

Pour the crème de cassis and lime juice (if using) into a sugared champagne
flute. Add champagne. Stir. MAKES 1 DRINK.

hot toddies

What could be more comforting when you come in from the cold than placing your hands around a glass filled with a steaming-hot, flavorful drink? As you take your first sip, the chill slips away and you feel relaxed and warm all over. Because hot toddies are made individually and not served from a communal bowl, it's a little tricky to serve them to a large crowd without letting them get cold.

You might consider putting all the ingredients on the table and allowing your guests to mix their toddies, minus the hot liquid, which you can pour yourself to avoid accidents.

Irish Coffee, page 51

nutcracker sweet

Just like its namesake, this comforting drink (pictured right) will make you think of the holidays. Grab a couple of shortbread cookies and sip it by the fire.

½ oz crème de cacao
½ oz amaretto
6 to 8 oz hot coffee

2 tbsp coffee ice cream
Almond shavings,
for garnish

Pour crème de cacao and amaretto into an Irish coffee glass. Add coffee to within an inch of rim. Stir until blended. Top with coffee ice cream and a few almond shavings. MAKES 1 DRINK.

hot buttered rum

Lore has it that in the 18th century, American politicians used this warm concoction to woo supporters. The butter adds a silky texture to this delightful classic.

1 tsp brown sugar
4 to 6 oz boiling water
1 tbsp butter

1½ oz dark rum
Freshly grated nutmeg,
for garnish

Put brown sugar into a glass punch cup and fill two-thirds full with boiling water. Add butter and rum. Wait until the butter melts, then stir and sprinkle a little nutmeg on top. MAKES 1 DRINK.

the blitzen

Even Santa has been known to sip on one of these after steering his sled through the cold, starry night.

1 oz Irish cream liqueur
1 oz dark rum
½ oz crème de cacao
8 oz hot chocolate
(page 70)

Whipped cream
(page 51)
Cocoa, for garnish

Pour Irish cream liqueur, dark rum, and crème de cacao into an Irish coffee glass. Add hot chocolate to within an inch of rim. Finish with whipped cream and add a dash of cocoa. MAKES 1 DRINK.

hot mint chocolate

After an evening of caroling, you can make plain hot chocolate for the kids and this Hot Mint Chocolate for the adults. It's a crowd pleaser . . . just make sure you've got enough candy canes to go around.

1 oz peppermint schnapps
8 oz hot chocolate
(page 70)

Mini candy cane

Pour peppermint schnapps into a glass mug. Fill to top with hot chocolate. Hang candy cane over side of glass. MAKES 1 DRINK.

irish coffee

You don't want to mess with this classic. It's best when prepared in the most traditional fashion, using Demerara sugar, a coarse raw sugar from Guyana. At many bars and restaurants, sugar is used to rim the glass, but for a true Irish Coffee, dissolve a couple of teaspoons of raw sugar into the drink.

2 tsp raw sugar, preferably Demerara sugar

1½ oz Irish whiskey

6 to 8 oz hot coffee

Whipped cream (see below)

Put the Demerara sugar in an Irish coffee glass. Add Irish whiskey and fill with coffee to within an inch of the rim. Cover surface to rim with whipped cream. MAKES 1 DRINK.

whipped cream

8 oz heavy (whipping) cream

1 tsp confectioners' sugar (optional)

Pour the cream into large bowl. If you want it sweetened, add sugar. Whip with electric or hand mixer until it peaks (be sure not to overwhip). Use immediately.

hot brandy alexander

Brandy is a delightful after-dinner drink, but if you're looking for something a little sweeter and a little richer, this is the drink for you. Dip biscotti into that pillowy whipped cream . . . this must be heaven.

4 oz milk

¾ oz brandy

¾ oz crème de cacao

Whipped cream (page 51)

Chocolate shavings,
for garnish

Heat the milk in a small saucepan over medium heat until very warm. Pour brandy and crème de cacao into a mug, then add the heated milk.
Stir until blended. Top with whipped cream and chocolate shavings.
MAKES 1 DRINK.

hot buttered apple cider

This yummy drink tastes like a melted toffee bar. Be sure to heat the cider until it's very hot. Try this buttery, rich drink with a crisp almond biscotti.

1 cup apple cider, heated

1½ oz butterscotch schnapps

Whipped cream, unsweetened (page 51)

Apple slice, for garnish

Pour very hot apple cider into an Irish coffee glass. Add butterscotch schnapps, then top with whipped cream. Garnish with apple slice. MAKES 1 DRINK.

hot buttered wine

This is a good alternative to the more potent Hot Buttered Rum (page 48). It's just as comforting and has a similar buttery flavor. The mingled scents of maple syrup and wine will soothe your nerves while the heat warms you.

¾ cup muscatel

⅛ cup water

1 tsp butter

2 tsp maple syrup

Freshly grated nutmeg,
    for garnish

Heat wine and water to just simmering; do not allow to boil. Preheat an Irish coffee glass with boiling water. Pour heated wine mixture into glass and add butter and maple syrup. Stir and sprinkle with a little nutmeg. MAKES 1 DRINK.

holiday punches

Punches are an easy way to serve a drink to a large crowd—just perfect for holiday get-togethers. The very sight of a punch bowl says "party," and the smells, colors, and flavors of these seasonal brews make any occasion festive. Their unpretentious charm also makes them good candidates for an afternoon open house or a casual potluck.

Wassail, page 62

'tis the season sangria

This version of the classic fruity punch is made with Cointreau, which adds a distinctive orange flavor. Sangria is traditionally served over ice but not here, since it can dilute the taste. (If you want to keep the sangria very cold, increase the recipe by half and freeze the extra in ice-cube trays.) The deep, rich red color of the punch makes it suitable for any kind of holiday gathering whether in afternoon or evening.

¼ cup sugar

1 cup water

Freshly squeezed juice of
   1 orange

Freshly squeezed juice of
   1 lemon

Cinnamon stick

750 ml red wine

1 oz Cointreau

6 oz sparkling water

4 oranges, thinly sliced,
   for garnish

½ lemon, thinly sliced,
   for garnish

½ lime, thinly sliced,
   for garnish

½ pippin or Granny Smith
   apple, cored and thinly
   sliced, for garnish

20 grapes, green and red,
   for garnish

Place sugar, water, orange and lemon juices, and cinnamon stick in a saucepan and bring to a boil. Reduce heat and simmer for 10 minutes. Remove from heat and let cool. Pour red wine, Cointreau, and sparkling water into a punch bowl. Remove cinnamon stick from the syrup, then pour into punch bowl. Float fruit on top. Chill for at least an hour before serving. MAKES 8 SERVINGS.

sparkling rose punch

This light punch is equally wonderful for a casual New Year's Day brunch or a gala holiday party. Its fresh, delicate flavor makes it a good accompaniment for all types of hors d'oeuvres, particularly those made with fish or shellfish. Serve it with steamed shrimp or oysters on the half shell.

6 tsp confectioners' sugar
  or sugar syrup (page 9)

1½ cups club soda

2 oz orange liqueur

4 oz brandy

4 cups chilled champagne

3 large mint sprigs,
  for garnish

20 to 25 pale pink rose
  petals (pesticide-free),
  for garnish

Fill medium-size punch bowl with ice. Add confectioners' sugar, club soda, orange liqueur, and brandy. Then add champagne and stir well. Garnish with mint and rose petals. MAKES 12 SERVINGS.

wassail

This traditional Norwegian punch gets its name from an old toast—it literally means "be in good health." Served warm, it's spicy with apple and brandy flavors and a beautiful pale amber hue.

Cinnamon stick

6 cloves

6 whole allspice berries

2 cups cranberry juice

6 cups apple cider

3 tbsp sugar syrup (page 9)

4 oz calvados

4 oz brandy

1 pippin or Granny Smith apple, quartered, cored and thinly sliced, for garnish

Wrap spices in cheesecloth and tie with string. Place cranberry juice, apple cider, sugar syrup, and spices in a stockpot, bring to a simmer, and cook for 8 to 10 minutes. Add calvados and brandy, and cook 1 to 2 minutes longer. Remove cheesecloth. Serve from heat-proof bowl into heat-proof cups—top each with a thin slice of apple. SERVES 8.

new year's day bloody mary punch

My mother is famous for her perfect Bloody Mary. Now the family secret is out! This recipe makes enough to serve a group.

4 cups Clamato

1 cup vodka

1 tsp Worcestershire sauce

1 tsp Tabasco

4 tsp creamed horseradish

Salt and freshly ground
 pepper

2 lemons, quartered

Combine Clamato, vodka, Worcestershire sauce, Tabasco, and horseradish in a large glass pitcher. Add salt and pepper to taste. Stir vigorously. Serve in tall highball glasses filled with ice. Squeeze lemon quarter over each drink and drop into glass. MAKES 8 SERVINGS.

jolly fruity cider

Use high-quality apple cider for the best flavor. Serve this punch alongside delicate Christmas sugar cookies and candied nuts.

1½ cups club soda

2 oz orange liqueur

4 oz brandy

4 cups apple cider

8 tsp confectioners' sugar or sugar syrup (page 9)

½ crisp red apple, quartered, cored, and thinly sliced

½ Bosc pear, quartered, cored, and thinly sliced

½ orange, thinly sliced into rounds

2 mint bunches, for garnish

Fill a large punch bowl with ice. Pour in club soda, orange liqueur, brandy, and apple cider. Add sugar, then stir vigorously. Float fruit on top. Serve in red wineglasses, or another glass with a wide rim, garnished with a mint sprig.

MAKES 12 SERVINGS.

sweet melted-snow punch

Sip on this wonderful beverage while snacking on holiday sweets, such as stollen, or a simple buttery Bundt cake.

10 cups milk

1½ cups malted milk powder

⅔ cup packed dark brown sugar

5 tsp vanilla extract

4 oz light rum

Cinnamon, for garnish

Pour milk into a large saucepan, and bring to a simmer. Whisk malted milk powder and brown sugar into simmering milk until dissolved, then stir in vanilla and rum. Pour into heatproof punch bowl or pitcher. Serve in prepared cups. Rim heatproof punch cups with cinnamon (see page 9). MAKES 10 SERVINGS.

glögg

This Scandinavian brew is sure to bring holiday cheer.

4 cups red wine

4 cups aquavit

Peel of 1 orange

Seeds from 2 cardamom pods

4 cloves

8 sugar cubes

Blanched whole almonds, for garnish

Raisins, for garnish

Place red wine and aquavit in separate saucepans and warm each over medium heat. Place orange peel, cardamom seeds, and cloves in the red wine, bring to a simmer, and cook for 10 minutes. Place the sugar cubes in a heated punch bowl, then add strained heated wine and the aquavit. In each heated mug place several almonds and raisins, then fill with Glögg and serve. SERVES 10 TO 12.

classic eggnog

This eggnog is creamy but not too rich, sweet but not cloying, and full-bodied without being too thick. Using real eggs, rather than an eggnog mix, makes an enormous difference in taste and texture. Real eggnog has fresh egg flavor and consistency, unlike many prepared varieties that are merely sweet and have the texture of watered-down pudding.

12 eggs, separated
¾ cup, plus 3 tbsp
    superfine sugar
3 cups milk

2 cups heavy whipping
    cream
1½ cups dark rum
Freshly grated nutmeg,
    for garnish

In a large mixing bowl, beat egg yolks well. Add the ¾ cup sugar and continue mixing until thick. Stir in milk, 1 cup cream, and rum. Cover and chill until cold. Beat egg whites until frothy, gradually adding the 3 tbsp sugar, then continue beating until soft peaks form. Fold egg whites and remaining 1 cup cream into cold yolk mixture. Ladle into glass punch cups or mugs and sprinkle with a little nutmeg. MAKES 24 SERVINGS.

Alcohol-Free Variation: Make without the rum, adding another cup of milk.

Note: Health officials have advised that eggs should not be consumed raw, particularly by those who are more vulnerable: pregnant and nursing mothers, invalids, and the elderly.

lively (nonalcoholic) libations

While planning a party, there's no reason to feel that drinks without alcohol are without distinction. I've made sure that these nonalcoholic drinks each have their own particular flavor and flair and are equally festive in appearance. You'll find a variety of choices from cold to hot to communal punches. For an alcohol-free variation of Classic Eggnog see page 67.

Shirley Temple, page 77

foamy mexican hot chocolate

Mexican hot chocolate usually comes in a round box with four ¾-inch disks of 8 wedges. The chocolate can be found in some supermarkets, specialty food stores, and Latin American groceries. It has a more complex taste and fragrance than your average hot chocolate, with hints of cinnamon, almonds, and vanilla. To serve with (or as) dessert, add marshmallows or a dollop of fresh whipped cream.

8 oz milk

2 wedges Mexican hot chocolate

marshmallows, for garnish

Heat milk in a small saucepan until very hot. In a blender, place the chocolate wedges and pulse until coarsely chopped. Add hot milk and blend until smooth. Serve in a mug, adding marshmallows for garnish. MAKES 1 DRINK.

gingersnap punch

This punch (pictured left) is popular with both kids and adults. Be sure to use fresh lime juice, or it won't have the necessary zip.

6 cups ginger ale

2 oz raspberry syrup

3 oz freshly squeezed
lime juice

8 candied lime slices, for
garnish (page 8)

Fill a large glass punch bowl with ice. Pour in ginger ale, raspberry syrup, and lime juice. Stir. Serve in a glass punch cup, garnished with a slice of candied lime. MAKES 8 SERVINGS.

cranberry sauce

This drink has lots of the ingredients that you might find in that seasonal relish we expect to see during the holidays.

6 oz cranberry cocktail

2 oz club soda

½ tsp freshly squeezed
lime juice

1 tsp freshly squeezed
orange juice

Lime twist, for garnish

Pour cranberry juice into a red wineglass filled with crushed ice. Add club soda and lime and orange juices, then stir. Garnish with lime twist. MAKES 1 DRINK.

hot vanilla cream

Looking for something cozy, like a pair of soft, fuzzy cashmere socks? If so, you'll enjoy this exceedingly subtle, gentle drink, perfect for dipping Christmas cookies.

8 oz milk

3 tbsp malted milk powder

1½ tsp vanilla extract

Whipped cream (page 51)

Freshly grated nutmeg, for garnish

Cinnamon, for garnish

Heat milk in a small saucepan until very hot. Add malted milk and vanilla, and whisk until slightly foamy. Pour into a mug and top with several dollops of whipped cream. Sprinkle with a little nutmeg and cinnamon. MAKES 1 DRINK.

mulled cider

Warm, fragrant, and delicious . . . a winter classic.

8 cups apple cider

2 tbsp maple syrup

Peel of 1 lemon

Peel of 1 orange

1 lemon, thinly sliced
into rounds

1 orange, thinly sliced into
rounds

2 tsp nutmeg

2 tsp cinnamon

2 cinnamon sticks

Pour cider and maple syrup into a large saucepan and bring to a simmer. Add all the remaining ingredients. Simmer for 15 minutes. Serve in heatproof punch cups. MAKES 16 SERVINGS.

partridge in a pear tree

There's no partridge, but this drink is full of pear flavor. The candied ginger adds a touch of sweet spice.

5 oz pear nectar

3 oz club soda

½ tsp freshly squeezed
lime juice

Gold leaf, for garnish

Piece of candied ginger,
for garnish

Pour pear nectar into a red wineglass filled with crushed ice. Add club soda and lime juice, and stir. Garnish with gold leaf and candied ginger. MAKES 1 DRINK.

shirley temple and roy rogers

There's not one child who doesn't adore this sweet "mocktail." Traditionally, the Shirley Temple (with ginger ale) is for girls, the Roy Rogers (with cola) for boys.

6 oz ginger ale or cola
1½ tsp grenadine
Orange slice, for garnish

Maraschino cherry,
for garnish

Pour ginger ale or cola into a red wineglass filled with crushed ice. Add grenadine and stir. Garnish with orange slice or maraschino cherry, as desired. MAKES 1 DRINK.

indexes

table of equivalents

The exact equivalents in the following tables have been rounded for convenience.

liquid/dry measures

U.S.	METRIC
¼ teaspoon	1.25 milliliters
½ teaspoon	2.5 milliliters
1 teaspoon	5 milliliters
1 tablespoon (3 teaspoons)	15 milliliters
1 fluid ounce (2 tablespoons)	30 milliliters
¼ cup	60 milliliters
⅓ cup	80 milliliters
½ cup	120 milliliters
1 cup	240 milliliters
1 pint (2 cups)	480 milliliters
1 quart (4 cups, 32 ounces)	960 milliliters
1 gallon (4 quarts)	3.84 liters
1 ounce (by weight)	28 grams
1 pound	454 grams
2.2 pounds	1 kilogram

length

U.S.	METRIC
⅛ inch	3 millimeters
¼ inch	6 millimeters
½ inch	12 millimeters
1 inch	2.5 centimeters

liquid measurements

1 dash	6 drops
1 tablespoon	½ ounce or 3 teaspoons
1 pony	1 ounce or 2 tablespoons
1 measure	1 ounce
1 jigger	1½ ounce or 3 tablespoons
1 large jigger	2 ounces or 4 tablespoons
¼ cup	2 ounces
½ cup	4 ounces
1 cup	8 ounces
1 pint	16 ounces or 2 cups
1 fifth (750 ml)	25.4 ounces (about 17 1½-ounce servings)
1 quart	32 ounces or 4 cups
1 liter (1000 ml)	33.8 ounces (about 22 1½-ounce servings)